I0389938

No Regrets!
Good+Bad=Great!

Devotis Lee

Edited by K. Lee

KLEPub.com

All rights reserved. No part of this book may be reproduced or transmitted in any form or by any means, electronic or mechanical, including photocopying, recording or any information storage and retrieval system without written permission of the publisher except for brief quotations used in reviews, written specifically for inclusion in a newspaper, blog, magazine, or academic paper.

Self Publishing services provided by Krystal Lee Enterprises (KLE Publishing) Copyright © 2022 by Devotis Lee. All rights reserved. Edited by K. Lee

Please send comments and questions:
Devotis Lee
Website: DevotisLee.com
IG: @dcafeandcatering
FB: @DCafeAtlanta
dcafeatlanta@gmail.com
Devotis@KLEPub.com

Krystal Lee Enterprises LLC
www.KLEPub.com   770-240-0089 Ext. 1
services@klepub.com or   sales@klepub.com
IG,FB: @KLEPUB

Printed in the United States of America.

ISBN: 978-1-945066-20-7

Dedication

Mom, I love you and I am forever indebted to you. To my husband and children, thank you for loving me through my life's changes. God, you are the reason that I live, breathe, and have everything I ever had. I am truly grateful for this journey. I have been blessed to experience life with everyone that I love, have loved, and hold dear.

Table Of Contents

Introduction...7

Chapter One...13

Chapter Two...21

Chapter Three...31

Chapter Four...43

Chapter Five...49

Chapter Six...55

Chapter Seven...63

Chapter Eight...71

Chapter Nine...79

Chapter Ten...87

Chapter Eleven...95

Chapter Twelve...103

About The Author...109

KLE Details...112

Introduction

Hopeless romantics exist in business just as in life. All of us want freedom, and our best life now, but there are only a few that will work for it. Perhaps that is the biggest divide between the haves and have-nots; the desire and will to make a decision to increase the trajectory of your life?

I know all too well that sheer willpower alone won't be enough to fight the adversity waiting on the other side of the door, in case you decide to open and look out the door of opportunity. What stops us from making the attempt? Is it for fear of what is on the other side of the door? Or do we bolt when we hit the slightest adversity?

The only more grave danger posed to our achievements is comfort. We get comfortable and focus on what we have, and this distraction blinds us to what can be obtained. Sometimes we exclude ourselves from having it. Yes, your internal conversations within yourself, could be the reason you never attempt to turn the doorknob for the door of opportunity.

You are not alone if you have--or will exclude yourself from envisioning a better life for yourself. We can have these mental blocks in our relationships, business, or pertaining to our physical and spiritual makeup. I too excluded myself from seeing better for myself, and it wasn't until I got fed up with the glass ceiling that I decided to break through it!

I had to stop and examine myself and ask the question, "What created that mindset, or lack of confidence in me?" One thing for sure, I knew something was lacking and I was determined to put my finger on it. Are you trying to put your finger on why you do the things you do? Why do you put up with ill-treatment on your job? Why do you allow the internal conversation to continue in your head that tells you, "You're not good enough?"

This voice didn't just magically have the power to have a heavy say in how you see and experience the world. Somewhere, someone gave it power and authority that you regard. The question we all must ask is, "Where did it come from and how can I access that area in my life to write a new narrative?"

The simple answer is it came from the company you keep. We are born into families that are a group outside of our control. Then we select our spouse, friends, and employer(s). You get to choose who and where you work along with the company you will keep.

Do you know that exposure to the right people can help us to know something else is out there? The right team around you can build you up or encourage self-sabotage. The wrong group of friends and spouse, can lead down a rabbit hole of failures and help to cure an insecure and self-doubting mindset.

Yes, if you can hire people, or create your team, you ought to do so by picking people that may intimidate you. An important key to selecting these people is ,"You have to be in the company that allows you to fail and not use it against you." You should be able to make mistakes, grow, learn, and teach others. The people that surround you should support you and also teach you.

I know I have posed many questions already within these few paragraphs, the big question on your mind right now maybe, "How do I build my team?" In the coming sections and chapters, I plan on telling you my story of how I escaped the mindset of exclusion. How I broke free of my comfort zone, and how I built up the team around me. As a bonus, I will show you how I continue to reach even beyond achieving my goals to accomplishing my dreams!

Some key aspects I must share with you are some of my challenges, advantages, and disadvantages that popped up along the way. To tell you this is a fix-all system would be shy of the truth. The truth, you will have to work for it, adjust, revamp, and push, but I assure you the work is worth it!

If I told you that my goal and passion to leave my mark on the world were not at the forefront of my mind when facing adversity, I would be misleading you. Ideally, I want to encourage the world to be a better place for my kids and grandchildren. You have to zero in on what matters to you. What can you not leave earth without doing? Then, that answer must drive you to make the best decisions, stay focused, believe in yourself, and keep your dream alive!

You don't have to be perfect, and you won't be—I wasn't and I am still learning. What I have found, however, you can be wonderfully flawed and still make it in due time if you don't give up. Your idea of success may change over the years, and that is ok. Never quit, never give up. Yes, you can do this, and I will help you start your journey by sharing with you my continued process.

Turn the page with me…

Chapter One

I was like you, working a job because I knew I had to stay alive and stay strong. Perhaps unlike some of you, I was married with grown children before I got the call to make a decision that would change my life! Or perhaps I got the call sooner, but I kept sending it to voicemail? Can you relate? Age does play a role in how we make decisions, doesn't it?

I give kudos to millennials for their ability to make leaping decisions, ones I would have seen as dangerous or too risky in my younger years. But before I spill the beans on my outburst while at work that eventually led me to entrepreneurship, it seems only fitting to explain some events leading up to this life decision.

I grew up with my mother, who was heavy on certain life principles. She raised me to respect my elders and remember "you never get anything free." Some of the biggest lessons my mom taught me shaped my life, I am sure likely shaped yours also, if you had an "old school momma." Let's scroll down memory lane for a bit—and for you millennials I ask for a bit of patience.

I spent the early years of my life not fully appreciating the value, structure, or understanding the foundation provided for me by my mother to live life. My mom did what she could to make sure we had food, shelter, and most importantly love. As I grew older I learned to be content with a little and I knew better than to ask for more than that. Did you have a mother too that could cut eyes and communicate without a word?

Good. I am glad I am not the only one; but as I started to get older and look back on my upbringing, I began to grow in understanding and appreciation of it. We had a-tracks that filled the house with music featuring stars that are now called legends, dead, or are no longer popular—but still relevant. We had chores to do and we seemed to clean up all day every day. We also had to address every adult we encountered as "sir" or "madam" no matter where we were from church to the grocery store.

Can you identify? Those were the rather simple lessons she taught me. The other more complex lessons, I didn't even realize became the building blocks for my thinking pattern well into my adult years. Those same values I also passed down to my children. Were you in a family that was so close-knit everyone regarded momma's word as law?

You know the family type that didn't dare ask questions, you just accepted whatever she said? It was like she had secrets that none of us knew as children—we didn't realize what she was sheltering us from and at the time we didn't appreciate it. Some of my friends didn't even know their mother's first name until third grade!

We were told things like "Stay in a child's place. Respect adult conversation and go play outside." She showed us how to appreciate being a kid, and most importantly being her child. She was protective over us and she made sure to let us know everything she did was for us and out of love. I didn't realize it then, but she taught us to trust her. We didn't ask questions, because we trusted she knew the reason. Do you have blind trust or faith in someone?

A critical aspect of my childhood that I could not ignore, that my mother again taught me and my siblings, is how to get along with enough. We were not poor, my mother worked in the hospital, but we were far from rich! She taught us a scriptural principle, to learn to be content in plenty—but especially if there is a want. Contentment I realized as I grew older wasn't to be confused with being complacent. Later I discovered, that when you learn to do better, do better.

Before I got that lesson under my belt, I was a master at living with what I had. I could make any conditions work in life. I was adaptable to my circumstances and I didn't think too much about changing that narrative. I was familiar with being reactive and not proactive. From the times of my youth to today, I didn't realize how much times had changed from my mother's day to the current. I now pay attention to that.

The sad part is that the very same lesson, to adapt, did prevent me from advancing as much as I should have early on. It is important to balance love and our ambition. There is nothing wrong with departmentalizing the wisdom of our ancestors, parents, and family to find new ways to make their advice relevant for the times that we live.

Raising my children and having a family, with my ambition, I realized the true balance and grace my mom had now that I am older more than I ever did in my youth. I no longer look back on my past and see the lack, but the abundance. I learned a method to use the abundant past for impacting my future and promoting my success.

I could say the same thing about my father. My father was a handsome and smart man. I often thought he would outthink his own best interest, perhaps he was willing to take too much risk. My dad was the type of man that having a family really didn't play a role in his life. His sights were set on providing this grand lifestyle for him to enjoy.

My father lived a busy life and didn't come around much. He was big into raffles, selling tickets, and passing as "white." He didn't come around much because he didn't want to be associated with black folks, or our struggles. I always felt cheated by his disappearance and often I wondered if he was ashamed of me?

I wished he would have come around more and told me more about himself. Most of what I know about him was told to me by my mother or other family members. It's amazing how we are born with the traits of our parents, but if they aren't present to help you maneuver some things, you are forced to learn your cope methods yourself.

When you have to do that, you take bumps and deal with life trials that could have been avoided if only you knew ahead of time. My memories are few and the stories my mom told me were limited also. I just knew he was witty, smart, and a businessman.

If I could share any advice on the subject, try

to nurture and establish relationships with those you can while you can. Our relationship was never perfect with me growing up, but I would have loved for that to be the case. I encourage anyone that has parents, who are still alive, to not forget about them and spend time with them whenever you can.

We don't know the day nor the hour, and we must not assume there will be a tomorrow. Yes, I loved my daddy, and I am grateful for his participation in bringing me life; I just wished he was around more to teach me how to live when I was younger.

Him chasing this lifestyle of money often left me and my siblings out of the loop. I loved him and wanted to get to know him, but his desire to make it big tended to leave us out. I would ask my siblings and even when I got older, did they want to connect with dad more? They all told me "no," and it was only me who thought about him and desired a relationship with him.

Sometimes we love people not because they were there for us, but because they brought us here. The warm and loving relationship I didn't have with my father growing up, but God gave us a chance to turn that around before he died. One of the best lessons I learned from my father was not to hate him for not being there for me.

I learned longsuffering, patience, and kindness from my relationship with my father. Instead of distancing myself, I came to his aid when he got deathly ill. I took this time as a way for him to get to know me and catch up on all the time I missed with him as a child.

It's amazing how God can redeem the time that was lost. Sometimes the best lesson we learn from someone is manifested in their absence. Yes, my dad was all about raffles and making big moves, and this hunger for prestige landed him in prison for a spell, but I did know he loved me. He would call and check in with me throughout my life and I was always grateful for that. His addiction wasn't drugs, but it surely was money.

I vowed not to let this hunger for success, money, and ambition destroy the relationship I wanted with and for my children. I discovered the secret to success was not in erasing my past, but in learning to embrace it. I vowed to pull out the best elements from all life accounts that could contribute to making me better. I wanted to eat the meat and spit out the bones as we used to say back in the day. Learning how to keep the good–or watch my perspective on how I viewed my experiences, helped me to reach for dreams.

Don't throw away anything that can make you better, and do reimagine, not that you lie to yourself about how you felt--how you feel; but make a conscious decision for how you want to process your past. Many of us never take the time to look at what hurt us and shaped us in our youth, but instead, we try to forget or ignore it. Don't fall into that trap and miss the pearl inside the clam.

You are never too old to look and learn from your past. At the kitchen table or in life, the saying is true and I pray that it helps you as it did for me. I have success and what some may consider failures, but it all made me who I am. Each step in front of me was determined in part by my past, so I learned to stop living in regret.

Another thing I like to say is don't live your life looking through the rearview mirror. When my father was done running and needed to rest. I remember taking care of him because I wanted our relationship to move forward.

I remember taking care of him for a few years before putting him in 24-hour care. For the last few years of his life, we enjoyed ourselves together and I was able to care for him until he died. I am glad I didn't spend my life hating him and I kept my heart open to love him and be loved. When he passed I had closure, peace, and before people leave this earth, try to get peace because when they are gone it maybe too late.

Chapter Two

Do you know your point of view does impact the possibilities you have? When we feel stuck in life, changing our point of view can help. Changing your view doesn't mean erasing what you see, but seeing what you see through different eyes.

A vantage point is another way to classify what we see. I like this word because it makes me think of the word advantage. Advantage is something you have over what others have. I believe my family gave me an advantage in life because I had to learn how to deal with difficult people. Love made us have to stay together, and our bond of family made us tighter. I am glad I wasn't the only child.

Growing up, I was afforded loving siblings that were better than expected, but yes we are brothers and sisters. We used to argue here and there, but we always looked out for each other. We had a house behind the projects, and our next-door neighbor was a strange man. He was a Peeping Tom to be more direct. He would scare me so badly that I hated walking past his house.

Some days I would look up and out the window and literally see him staring at me. I am not saying he had cruel intentions for me specifically, but he was always looking in our windows. He would be peeking through bushes, trees, and all sorts of things to watch us. It is an unsettling feeling to look up and lock eyes with someone staring at you through the window. Catching him in the act always gave me the "heebee jeebies."

This was nothing cute like in the movies when some good-looking guy–your age has a crush on you, but a creepy, icky way that keeps you awake at night. My older sister always made me feel safe going home on the trail—and my stepfather didn't play either. I thought the two of them might get into a fight a few times, but thankfully that didn't happen. He was a fantastic guy and I loved him, my stepfather. Of course, my other sister also did her best to make me feel safe as well. I was grateful for them all, and happier when we moved from there.

To be honest, and not beat a dead horse, which is a terrible saying I remember hearing as a child. I am not sure how old of a saying it is though.

I always appreciated my stepdad, but his presence and love did make me miss my father more at times. I would feel bad sometimes because I knew it wasn't fair, but he was such a good man and would always comfort me about it. To be frank, I knew my dad in bits and pieces, but this man was more like my father growing up.

I will always be grateful for him, but he wasn't the only one that protected me growing up. My sister and mother also felt responsible for developing me socially. I remember that my mother and older sister would talk to me and teach me fundamental basics about fashion, hair, and such. My sisters were so pretty (as was my mom), and they always dressed nice. My older sister was the ring leader and her hair was always done. The two of them looked like brown porcelain dolls when it came to style.

I am sure my mom was gorgeous, and in style with the popular fashions of her day, but my sister and I could relate more. We were closer in age and fashion sense so I leaned on both of them a lot. Our mother supported us and how we bonded together. She was a seamstress for us and she always made our dresses according to our style. I would not have imagined that today it would be cheaper to go into a store and buy something off the rack than to make something at home, but here we are!

I have to admit, I did not have the same

confidence in wearing everything like my sisters could. Not that we were different in taste or size, but because I had scars that they didn't. Kids can be so cruel; and at my elementary school, in a very small town in Pennsylvania that only grew popular because of Tony Dorsett, I was teased constantly. Yes, I was raised with the amazing superstar Tony Dorsett. He was loved by our town, but for me, I didn't get the royal treatment.

My memory for most of the kids I grew up with was dreadful as some of the white children (who predominantly lived in the area) thought it funny to nickname me "torch." I hated it. I despised the name so much that I dare not show them another scar beyond the burn marks visible on my hand. I didn't want to encourage any more ridicule or laughter. I failed PE because I refused to dress down and expose the scars on my legs.

When I was about 9 months old I was burned pretty badly on my arm and hand. The skin was grafted from my leg, and unfortunately, it wasn't done well. Not sure if it was a money thing, race, or my size, but I became self-conscious about my scar ever since. My elementary years were the most difficult years dealing with the embarrassment of my scars.

My mom was so protective over me because of that too I think. I could never bring myself to tell her any pain I was in because I saw how hard she worked to keep everything together. I knew it would have broken her heart for her to think she failed us in any way.

But I came to realize later, that sometimes we have to pop a person's bubble, because keeping them out of the loop may cause more damage. I did fear the outcome of telling her a close relative violated me as a child. I was unsure if she would go ballistic or have thoughts that would torment or kill her on the inside (or someone else). I thought I was protecting her.

I didn't tell her until I was 35 about what happened to me. We were both kids at the time and I honestly thought time would heal it. You've heard the saying, time heals all things. Well, that simply isn't true. Like you–you too were probably raised to protect your family; I didn't know or understand what that meant when I was a child. I did what I thought was best and never told anyone.

Unfortunately, as I grew older, I realized pinned-up hurt, pain, or shame can always make headway—and it did. Too many times I was brought to tears or extreme emotions concerning the matter, but I didn't know what to do after. I remember going to my grandfather's funeral sometime after it happened. Ironically, if I would have told anyone what happened to me at the time, it would have been my grandfather.

I remember going to his casket wanting to tell him, and even go live with him and my grandmother after it happened. I always felt loved and cared for by them. I didn't know how to face what I was going through, so I thought to run somewhere I felt safe. Unfortunately, it wasn't at home, not in this city, and not at school. But I didn't tell my grandfather who lay in the casket covered in what looked like wax.

I wasn't ready to know the outcome of my secret until I told my mother as an adult. She was concerned, she cried with me; she asked why I didn't tell her sooner, I didn't have a real excuse I realized at 35. It was at that moment, grown, after burying it for so long, I was made free from it. After it came out and I confronted my pain, frustration, and anger I could start healing from it.

There is something that happens when you talk about it. My tip, if something is hurting—or bothering you, always speak up for yourself even if you think it would put you at odds with someone else. Your loyalty to your family, should not cost your virtue. A secret should not cause pain because it was buried, and the only true way to move on is to heal. You need to heal so you can get free and overcome it because forgetting about it is not realistic or possible.

I remember when we left that small town to move back to Atlanta, I was born in Atlanta on Oct

11, 1957. We were returning home After my grandfather had passed, he left my grandmother behind in the house alone. She would come to visit us all the time in Pennsylvania when my grandfather was alive. Things changed a lot when my grandfather died.

My mother came to realize, now, her mother needed her; I think even all of us to keep her company. I may have picked on my siblings from time to time, but it was only because I wanted to be just like them. I love my sisters and brothers, and we all loved our grandmother. We wanted to support her and it was a no-brainer to move to Atlanta for most of us.

My grandmother sent us a moving truck for the move from Pennsylvania to Atlanta Georgia. My uncles came together to pack us up and drive our things down. My stepfather moved with us, but he and my mom split sometime later. I remember my older sister decided to stay in Washington because she had a decent job babysitting children; so it was my other sister and I who moved with my mom.

My sister and I didn't drive down in the truck or our car, but we traveled by train. I loved the train, but my mother did not have the most memorable trip. traveling in the truck with my uncles. I had a dog named "Scottie," and my mother was always afraid of him. She loved us so much that she allowed us to keep him.

She didn't as much as pet the dog let alone hold him before this trip. On the move down she did the unthinkable and held him for the entire trip down. Surely that was love and the product of it—courage! To hold your fear in your arms—and like it, because you knew it would mean the world to someone else... powerful.

The lesson here is love doesn't make you weak, but powerful and full of courage to achieve the unthinkable. So we arrived in Atlanta and wow, what a different picture. This city opened up a whole new world for me. I felt like a fish out of water walking on land!

When we are introduced to new things, although we may believe we won't change, oftentimes we do—and sometimes by a lot. When in Pennsylvania I loved to read. I wore long dresses and pants to hide my scars. The kids in Atlanta were different and way more welcoming than those back in Pennsylvania. I went to a predominately all-white school, but in chocolate city, that changed.

My scar was no longer a laughing matter but a positive talking point. I went from unpopular, and only noticeable to many for a good laugh, to being a friend to the most desirable people in school. I couldn't read anymore, because I made no time for it. I had way more on my mind and on my schedule than sitting home and reading books!

When in Pennsylvania I read mystery books with a female detective that would keep me entertained for hours. I was truly a bookworm reading whatever my mom bought for me and I was grateful. In this city, reading just felt less entertaining than the trouble I could get into with my friends and going around the city.

In Atlanta like PA, we didn't live in the ghetto or projects; but we weren't too far away from it either. I really had every excuse to live life right and make the right decisions. I remember my grandmother would bring me to Buckhead with her and show me the fine homes she was charged with cleaning and maintaining. She taught me how to set the table for fine dining, polish silverware, and keep a lovely home.

I also remember attending my first ball! Oh, how I loved putting on my dress, getting dolled up, and feeling important. I was a lucky girl to have been invited to a grand hotel to hang out with influential and affluent people. I felt empowered, may be entitled humbly speaking, to achieve great things in my life. I wanted this to last.

I wanted to feel this love, wear nice clothes, look great, and feel incredible, all the days of my life. I wasn't sure what that would require, but I was determined to live a life worthy of my existence and be proud of who I am. My grandmother may have appeared simple to some, working as a maid, but she showed me that grand things can come to those that work hard and keep their head up. This woman taught me how to be proud without being full of pride.

Chapter Three

My early years with my mom, siblings, uncles, grandmother, and everyone else was a testing ground for life. I wasn't sure where life would take me, but like you, I knew it would be a great place. I wanted so badly to be impressive and to earn my mother's approval all my life; even more, as I grew older.

I was not a perfect teenager although my mom would have argued differently if she were alive to tell it. She said the most beautiful and profound words to me, and all my siblings, in a letter she had us read after her passing. She wrote to us, "none of my children have disappointed me."

Moms are supposed to be forgiving and I expected to hear how she loved me while alive, but there was something deep to her words after her passing. I needed to hear them the most then. High school was scary, I don't think it matters where you live. I was not as sure of myself as the other kids, because unlike my classmates, coming to Atlanta was where I first started feeling like I fit in. This was the first time I attended school and most of the kids looked like me.

I was always a good student no matter what school I attended. I was asked to help the teacher all the time, run errands for them, and complete tasks. I am not sure if at the previous schools that was all in good faith at the moment, but we will assume it was well-intended. In high school, I didn't want to be a bookworm if that meant being left out of the happenings.

I wanted to be in the in-crowd, because if you are not, who are you? I know when we get older we don't think like this, but as a high schooler, this is everything. Having friends and not being left out is what we all craved. We wanted attention, friendships, and maybe to have someone that admired us. Deep down, we all want to feel and believe we are special.

My high school was like any other. There were jocks, and determining factors for how cool you are, and places you wanted to be. My first two years were not all that impressive. I had a few close friends. We worked together to keep our grades up and get into a little bit of trouble but nothing major. It wasn't until I was 16 that I thought of upping the ante.

I felt I was ready to date. Not sure how I got to this decision, or if it was because I had caught the attention of the most popular boy in school. Every girl wanted to be me, but did they really? I didn't realize what it meant to be his girlfriend. I had to go where he went, do what he did, and yet suffer a different consequence.

You see when you are believed to be a pro athlete potential, every door is opened to you. You can do no wrong. You can miss school, and it does not count against you. You can flunk tests and no one notices. You can come to school for practice, and then go home and be marked present in every class. His treatment was not the same for me.

I was skipping school with him, but my attendance reflected my absences while he was marked present. I should have realized the rules of the game are lopsided in some people's favor early on. My tip, which I wished I had gotten back then, is that if the game is rigged, if you break the rules or step outside the box, make every step count! I wasn't focused on the box, because I thought love was more important. I thought my commitment to him, put me outside the box.

I missed some fundamental truth about

that box clearly when I was younger that I did find out about a year later. Surely today I am even more familiar with the boxes people try to place you in. When you think outside the box, and do what has never been done—or shouldn't be done in some cases, you don't want it to negatively impact you or rob you of your freedom. While in this relationship, I did everything I was big and bad enough to do. The only thing that stopped me and forced me to look at my choices was when I ended up pregnant at 16.

During the '70s and '80s, it was not socially tolerable to be pregnant in high school. They (the school) would put you out and make you attend night school. The school or parents believed the girls getting pregnant would be a negative influence on their peers. So they would remove you from your classes and make you enroll in a down-low educational program.

The treatment of young girls pregnant by sports stars of the school was even worse. It was like my presence and girls like me were a stigma against the entire school. We were the blame for this potential superstar failing or getting distracted. We were a mark that was so quickly put away. It was as if they put me away and threw away the key into the sea of forgetfulness.

I was a social butterfly, who enjoyed parties, going places, dancing, smiling, and laughing with my friends. I stopped reading books to be out and about, and at this time I felt like a caged bird. Reading no longer seemed as enjoyable because it felt like a prison. Reading was the last resort to be entertained not a willful choice for me anymore. At this time of my life, I cried a lot because I felt lonely and rejected.

I had planned to attend prom and other school dances, but I couldn't go. I realized the ball I went to some years ago would be the closest I would get to a prom. I became a stigma that other parents pointed their fingers at and attempted to judge my mother. I felt so bad for how I seemingly repaid my mother for her love and support over the years.

You would have thought I was scum the way some mothers recoiled their daughters from my friendship. I would never call my children a mistake, and I thank God every day that my mother didn't either. It was never a choice on if I would continue with my pregnancy, it was a no-brainer for me and my mother. Really my whole family!

At the age of 17, I thought I knew enough to make the biggest decision, and pivotal choice to start a family. Sure I didn't think it all the way through and plan out the details. When it happened though, I knew this was the way I had to go even if everything was cloudy. I cried many nights, but I wasn't going to allow anyone to shove me into a box and treat me as if I didn't matter.

At this moment, my world slowed down and books, family, started to find more room on my calendar. I was still a young adult, child, teenager, trying to figure myself out. So many things, experiences I would never have because I took this road instead of another; but this time stepping outside the box I was going to make it work for me!

I was determined to finish high school and I did. The young man I had my son with, I married after high school. We went on to have two more children. He went to college and had hopes of playing in the NFL, but he couldn't adjust from being a school superstar to a college rookie. He didn't get the passes or play the game as well as he did in high school. He didn't live life or play the game as well when the playing field was no longer lopsided in his favor.

My tip, nothing hits harder than having a chance at greatness and realizing you are unprepared for the breakthrough and opportunity! Had my first son not put the breaks on my running wild, maybe I would have missed the mark too? I didn't think at the time hitting the mark meant stepping outside the box to have a child. Then, that child being the reason I would be more careful and calculated with my choices.

I wasn't able to go to college in the traditional sense, but I made a way. My mom helped in ways she could. My uncle stepped up big time by putting a playpen at his real estate office to watch my son while I went to school to pursue my college degree. My husband was the least supportive of my choices and became cruel, bitter, and hard to live with. He motivated me to embrace another taboo, divorce.

No one can truly understand why we make the decisions we make, and perhaps it is unfair to expect them to get it. One thing I do believe we all should pray for is that people would respect our decisions. My mother always did that for me. I didn't know everything but I knew the importance of education and I refused to allow my son to become an excuse for me not getting to where I wanted to be in life. I chose to make him a blessing to me, a motivation, and not a weight.

So I did in life what all young black women and men were told to do, build up their education and go seek a job. My mom gave us the very best life advice based on her experience. She worked every day to take care of us. She didn't let anything stop her from being on time, working with pride, and taking what she has made to provide for us.

I loved her for teaching me hard work, but to be honest, she didn't teach me everything about how to work smart. I went to night school, and during that time I put all my effort into making good grades in my last year of high school. I wasn't the most reliable student in class, especially before my senior year, but amazingly I was able to pull on that work ethic to get a job.

Getting that first job was a sweet accomplishment that allowed me to give back to my children and family. I was so proud. Yes, I know a degree is important, but I saw it as a means to an end after I addressed my imminent concerns. Taking care of my children and myself was always the most important thing in my life. My family trumped my dreams and aspirations. At this time I didn't see how the two could be aligned, but I knew one day I would!

I became a bartender at a local restaurant. For the interview, I was dressed and ready to work. I believe in first impressions, so I was on time, and they asked the dreaded question we all hate. How are you qualified? Ironically, how can I be qualified if I never tried and if I don't get a chance to try, how can I become qualified? I had never served a drink in my life before getting this job. I was not prepared at the time, but I was committed to doing whatever I needed to, to become successful in this job.

I got the job as I set out to do, and I headed straight for the library after. I know we live in a world where phones are the new library, but in my day, we had to come to this building. Who would have thought reading would instantly come back in handy? I spent the entire day at the library looking at books, reading about drinks, instructions, recipes, and the like. On my first day, I was nervous and relied heavily on good conversation to pull me through.

The job got easier and the money swelled to what would have been a comfortable life, but I wanted more. I wanted a career. I would like to spend more time with my children and not work such late shifts. I sought out a few day jobs that I worked temporarily. The job that stuck was the post office.

Working for the post office seemed like the job for me to retire at. During the '80s and '90s, they were the most stable position a black person could get. It was here I met my second husband and many friends. It was hard raising the children by myself, but every day was worth it. This wonderful man was a blessing to me and my children. I love him still, and yes, we have been through a lot together. He has been and continues to be my greatest support.

About the post office, a recurring theme in my life came back to raise its head again. My aunt had passed away and my husband and I both wanted to go to her funeral. Of course, we both had to apply for the day off for the same reason. Strangely enough, they approved his request but rejected my time. They claimed too many people would be out of the office. I remember thinking, how could I have stayed and missed my aunt's funeral? So I went anyway and of course, I was let go while he kept his job.

I was grateful that he kept his job, but I felt it was very biased against me. We needed two incomes to support our family. We had 5 children and bills that seemed non-stop. It is like the universe knows when someone loses a job, and the enemy says to raise the prices. It felt like everything was going up except our income. If we were cruising by before, the road is getting a whole lot bumpier now.

I remember when I applied to this prominent packaging and shipping company. At this company, I was very uncertain if I would be qualified to work for the position I applied for, but I did it anyway. Up until this point, I still hadn't completed my degree, but I needed a job! I desired to go back to school, but life seemed more important again. Paying bills, taking care of children, and spending time with loved ones filled our lives. I couldn't put another bill on my husband and strain my family more.

I was so busy looking for a job and doing family stuff, I had no time to think to see any life term goals realized. I was fueled by the here and now. My husband prepared me for challenges as best he could. It just came a time, that he had to encourage me to lean on God and not him for everything. I had to get to know God for us to maintain and move forward in life. I was the one that was changing the dynamics of the family and I was feeling the aftermath of that.

I learned a valuable lesson about prayer and God's promises. I had to learn to mix faith with action and not lean on desperation and emotions to pull me through. Crying got me through high school drama, but prayer got me through this.

Chapter Four

I remember thinking, "How does anyone expect me to get a job in a profession if I first must have the experience to qualify. Truly this is a catch-22 for the elite. A sick, twisted game to keep certain people out and the in-crowd on top!" I felt the corporate ladder was rigged, but rigged or not, I had to make it. I had to do my very best like my mother and siblings, my husband and children are expecting me too.

I remember when I went to my interview. I spent at least 30 minutes in the mirror mastering my outfit alone. I knew every color, and detail was a representation not only of me but everyone that ever did something for me. Talk about the pressure! It's crazy, but the way you speak, the words you say, and how you carry yourself say a lot about how you were raised, and how you would work for someone if hired!

Being a good representation of a company's brand is paramount and I do understand it. I had to be the best, even better than the rest because I had no experience. I didn't have the hook-up for the interview either. Everything was cold turkey, just me and God.

The only thing that kept me within my skin, was my faith in God. Amazing how when we feel as if we don't measure up, God can show us how He is bigger than the difficulty or emotions we feel. I had to push all my nerves aside and remember, "I got this!" I am sure you can relate? When we get to the point where being cute is not enough and we have to get real—I was there.

I wasn't letting anything stand in my way and God would not keep anything from me that I needed to survive. So after 30 minutes in the mirror, praying myself up to get this job, I was now ready to face the powers that be. Of course after putting my shoes on, eating breakfast, sending my kids off to school, and wishing my husband well at work. A woman's job is so complex, yet the Father gives us the grace to manage it every day doesn't He?

I prayed as I drove and listened to worship music to keep me in good spirits. I arrived full of the Holy Ghost! I grew up in the church, but there is no growth like growing in the season of adversity. So this was my next Goliath, not the job, but joblessness. God helped me to slay it on this day.

The interview appeared to go well. I was a social talker, and working with the mail company prepared me in many ways for the interview. I knew the business. I flowed in conversation in this area, the challenge was I was working in a computer system I had never seen before.

I am not a stupid person I would like to think, but there are some habits I have long had. I have always struggled with something that made me ask the question is something wrong with me? You know when you have to read something more than once, and more than twice to understand it. I struggled with comprehension, but only for certain things that I read.

I thought for a while I was a loner in this area. I remember in school I also struggled with reading math questions, or instructions sometimes. I was always committed to learning what I needed to, so I would go the extra mile. So reading something four and five times, I would do to understand. I have to admit, I did beat myself up mentally because I felt it was something I shouldn't have had to do.

It wasn't until I got to Corporate America,

that I realized other people had to do the same thing. It is not as unfamiliar as I had originally thought. I didn't recognize this condition existed in other people because I was too busy only looking and beating myself up. During presentations, and training with other new hires, I realized we were all struggling and doing similar things.

I was struggling in the beginning to catch on to new material. I signed up for every program I could find to help me prepare for this position. I refused to be outdone and what I learned I shared with others also facing challenges. I believe we are blessed to achieve and are gifted to bless others. A servant attitude I didn't realize was building in me and setting the pace for leadership in my near future.

Before anyone can lead, they first must be lead. We have to get in a position to learn and be taught. Then we have to desire to help others if we want to be successful at being good leaders. I saw that God's faithfulness isn't simply praying and expecting Him to do all the work. It starts with faith that moves us to act, and then the Father moves to help stretch our abilities to achieve greatness.

I would have never believed I would have the time to get my degree with everything on my plate—but I did. I didn't know what kind of mother I would be with this job. Working full-time in a corporate setting can tend to take over your life. I did feel guilty at times realizing how much time I spent at the office each week.

I made sure to balance my time outside the office with going to my children's sports games. I was active in the school's PTA, I even made sure they went to school and had what they needed. I did not spoil my children with fancy things, but I bought them quality items to keep them on track. My husband and I worked as a team to provide and take care of our children.

We sacrificed a lot for them that at times we didn't make as much time for each other. I knew this trap of limited affection would come back to haunt us. So many marriages seem to be torn up slowly over time because we overlook simple things for keeping the marriage in good health. We have to understand setting time aside for each other is also family time.

I didn't realize I was giving so much energy to work and our youngsters, that I didn't have much energy for my husband. We functioned as agreeable roommates for the most part, but we forgot to have fun with one another. I worked In Corporate America for over 15 years. I remember when I started the position I was part-time and they told me most people didn't become full-time for 10 years.

I reached full time within 2 years and while working here I was blessed with stable employment.

I saw the window to complete my degree in ministry and I didn't hesitate to complete it. Getting ordained at graduation was so special to me and I enjoy being involved with the church. I still plan on getting my master's in business at some point, but I am pleased to have earned my degree in Organizational Leadership Management.

    I was used to giving my all, so I found myself really confused when it all came to a crashing halt and my life changed forever.

Chapter Five

So life would appear to be going great! I got the degree I had been pushing for. I was working with a great company, married, enjoying my children, and living the dream. Or so it would appear, but the truth was my relationships were strained.

Ever since I had my children, everything I did, working especially, getting married, earning my degree, I did for them. I wanted to be a good example. I wanted to show them everything I wanted them to have and become. My mom stressed a good education and I wanted to show her that I would follow in her direction and get an education.

We had so many breaks because she worked in the hospital industry. She did stress job security and I learned to appreciate that too. I wanted her to know, my grandmother, and uncle who helped a lot too that they didn't waste their time

I didn't realize how what I was chasing to help them was also taken from me. I lost some time to spend with them and perhaps be there for them. Going to work I sometimes thought I should be doing more for them, but I had to choose.

While I was getting my degree my marriage took one of the drastic turns for the worst in our marriage thus far. Like in many marriages that have over a decade under their belt, we get comfortable and assume things will stay the same no matter what. We get reliant on our partner and never think they will leave.

As I was running and doing, I knew he loved me, and I loved him. But I didn't think I had to win him over anymore. Date night was something honestly I stopped planning for. I couldn't even remember our last vacation. We had been in love after all this time, how could that truth be missed? In pursuit of what I wanted, I did have to sacrifice time here and there and it was stressful.

But I didn't realize how being a bit selfish for my own dreams would mean I took my eye off my family. During my studies, one of my sons spent some time in jail. My husband and I were arguing all the time, and it was because of my ambition and lack of time. I knew something had to change but I wasn't sure how to stop the machine.

My son had something similar to say while he was in prison. I didn't agree, but I understood. Sometimes the sacrifice is not worth the trouble that follows, but often it is. I had to get back to the basics of family first, but I also wanted my dream also!

As we change, not everyone may be on board at the time. They are used to who you were and accustomed to how you have been. When you change that, it is something to get used to; and surely something to talk about. I didn't do much talking about my changes. I kind of made up my mind and then I went for it. I am still working to better communicate because I think there is always room to improve.

I knew my husband and I needed to talk. He had to understand who I am today, not just accept who I was. I am growing and I want him to be here with me. I want him to understand how he fits into my life before, and how he still fits now. I often wondered is it ever fair to change, or grow, when someone married you for who you were then?

With my degree, I grew closer to God, the closest I had ever been up until this point in my life–and I needed it. It seems like the closer we get to something worth having, the more opposition comes. It comes to test you on if you believe or truly want what you're going after. Don't be afraid to fight. Fight for your children, your marriage, your career, your purpose, or whatever it is you desire.

The Bible says that God will give us the desires of our hearts, but do we believe that? My desire was to stay married, help my children, and grow in my career. I had not given up on that just because I got older. I am still here, so my life is still relevant–and so is yours.

Like anything, if you put off the necessary changes, you find that there is some work to do. To get my marriage back on track, I had to go to counseling to learn how to better communicate. I need to work through my pain and frustration with the marriage. I also knew he had justifiable needs as well. I realized I didn't know how to do it all by myself. The two of us talking together didn't fix everything. We didn't have the best marriage, but I wanted us to hold on to what we did have despite the challenges.

I was a giver, and not to say my husband was not, but I needed to see why I was giving to people. Sometimes people that are close to you can try and manipulate you into giving. I had to learn giving out of compulsion is also just as damaging as not giving at all. I need balance and I needed help to do it.

I also realized I needed to work more at expressing my real thoughts uncensored. The more we outlined our individual problems or issues, it helped us to recommit ourselves to the marriage and be reminded we were a team. We had to put us being a great pair back into perspective and lock it in to make sure divorce was not on the table. Securing my marriage is my first priority after loving God and together we care for our children.

We are a family and we stick together in tough and good times. Together we had accomplished so much. He is the reason I could go back to school, stay at this job, and accomplish what I have while with him. My goal was to allow God to give us beauty for ashes. He turned around my marriage first, but we both had to put the work in to work with God to restore what had been neglected.

Our son, who was in trouble, inspired me to give back and volunteer at the jail and prison to teach life skills. I would have never thought to give back in this way had he not gotten into trouble. I never thought of the people that get caught up in life, because I was busy focusing on myself. I had to learn, that you can accomplish your goals or dreams and still make time for what matters. You simply have to be open to taking a detour and allowing those you care about to change how you accomplish your goals.

I believe in paying it forward no matter where you are in life. Someone is always having a tough time or going through that could use your help. As you grow, you want your community to grow with you. I will further explain later in this book, but first, after I got my marriage on track, given back on account of my son, lastly, I turn to my job.

My job at this point I had worked for 17 years. I have seen people come and grow from my department and many of those people I had trained. It has always been my desire to obtain a position in management and not simply be the go-to employee for new people.

Chapter Six

Waking up in the ambulance seemed like a sweet place to be from where I just left. It is nothing like feeling like the hard work and loyalty you gave were completely overlooked. Nothing feels like corporate America hurt.

I felt so lucky and blessed to have this job. I appreciated the simple things that God allowed me to experience and learn. I realized at some point I hit a glass ceiling and I wasn't sure when I did. Perhaps it had been years ago–but I was comfortable and didn't notice.

This day was like the slap that woke me up out of my sleep and boy did I land hard! I heard the paramedics talk with each other as I lay there helplessly. I couldn't help but think as I was receiving oxygen. Father, I need you to breathe new life into my dreams. I need direction and I need healing.

Somehow I forgot about the little girl inside of me that dreamed about being an FBI agent. Sure, the time has passed to pursue this career but not to make an impact. I wanted to do something with my life to help people and feel like I am leaving something behind not only for my children but also for my community.

I am more than a worker-bee, I am a woman, mother, wife, and community influencer. Since I could remember, my friends and I who kept in touch since middle school talked about our desires and life goals. Of the three of us that are still close, it is a blessing to see how God gave us what we spoke about so many years ago.

We said we wanted to get married, work jobs, take care of our family, and stay friends until we die. Good thing we are still living and following our plans; but I can't say everyone I knew kept up their dreams. So many of those girls and parents that looked down on me when I had my son in high school were nowhere to be found.

Many of their daughters ended up on drugs, dying so much earlier than their time. I realized what you did yesterday truly doesn't dictate what you are going to be doing tomorrow. I would have never thought so many would have gotten caught up like they did.

But they helped me realize while I was lying on the stretcher, the decisions I make moving forward will either take me closer to my future or send me to an early grave. I wasn't as young as I used to be, but surely my time was not yet up! There was more I desired to do and I was set on accomplishing it.

I still had a husband and children I wanted to see get older. I had to fight and find a reason worth fighting for. Have you ever had a life or death decision to make? Sometimes these decisions are simple questions like are you going to keep pretending the choices and actions you are making don't really matter? Living or working here really doesn't negate your plans, but you are resenting every moment of your life.

The life you lived that used to be fun and funny, now seems like a burden, boring, or predictable. You need a change, a vacation even, an equal need might be rest. But how can you get that when you have to keep the engine of life running? Bills are still due, obligations still have to be met, so you keep going thinking of the bigger picture.

I had to start thinking of the big picture when my life was interrupted unexpectedly. I had a choice to make not only about my health but my life. I couldn't help but think when I was sitting in the hospital recovering. I had to choose to live, take care of myself, and that meant valuing myself!

Are you guilty of seeing the worth in everything and everyone excluding yourself–or those that are the closest to you? I wasn't at every game for my children and realized why my marriage struggled a bit too. I was working to help with finances and such, but I was merely surviving! I realized it wasn't too late to live, just because I had gotten older. I still have breath in my lungs, and now I choose to start living finally.

I wanted a lifestyle that would allow me to be there for my family and enjoy the time with my grandchildren that I was missing with my own children. I guess this was like a second chance for me to live the life I had always dreamed of. Honestly, I never really thought about what I wanted to do since high school besides getting a job, going to school, and working in the church.

When I got home, my husband didn't push me and my job did their best to hold my chair until I was ready to come back to work. They called me several times, but I just had no interest or desire to return. I knew when I ended up in the ambulance I never wanted to come back, but what would I do next?

I remember the phone rang and I looked at it. I knew who it was but I didn't want to talk. My husband picked up the receiver and my new boss was on the other end. "Mr. Lee, we really need to speak with your wife. We understand she underwent a serious ordeal and we are wanting to be here for her, but we have waited several months to get a date for her expected return."

She continued to say, "If we do not hear from her soon, we will assume she has decided not to return. Again, we understand if this is the choice Mrs. Lee has determined to make, but we would love it if she would return. Kindly give her our message and ask her to call us back in the next few days. If we don't hear back, we will start looking for her replacement. Thanks so much for your time."

I was close and within earshot. I heard every word. I know it was meant to be kind, and thoughtful, but it felt just as icy as the hospital room I had left. I had ideas dancing around in my head, but one thing was decided, I am not going back. When my husband hung up the phone he looked at me, "You know you are going to have to tell them when you are going back to work?"

"What if I don't want to return? I mean what if I want to do something else?"

"Like what?" He said.

"Maybe go back to school, study business, or start my own business?"

"Don't you think we are a bit old to try a different career? We are almost able to retire, why should we start over?"

"If not now, then when? I always wanted to have my own business, maybe I can do that?"

"I can't tell you what to do, and if I tried you wouldn't listen anyway. Just talk to me before you make any decisions."

"Okay."

"And before you call your job back and tell them you officially quit, think through some of the details on what kind of business you want to start. Please…"

"Okay, I will let you know."

"I'm not going to lie, I am not saying this is a great idea. I understand your health, but I don't know if starting a business right now is what we should be doing. I mean this is a lot of work and risk–and at a bad time. You just left the hospital not too long ago. Can you handle the stress of all this?"

Yes, marriage is hard work. There is always one that tends to give more than the other. One that has to be bigger, and stick it out, when times are rough. You find that both parties have to give to make it work. We just give different things because the answer is often not divorcing or walking away.

We both had to choose that our marriage was worth fighting for because the decision I was making was not easy. It hurt that he didn't have the response I wanted him to. I am sure he knew of the pressure coming his way if starting this business failed. I couldn't think of that though, failing.

We didn't look at me starting a business the same way, but we both remained committed to each other. We have learned over the years, that neither one of us is perfect. He was right about a few things too with starting my business. The call into my job was not easy, not that I didn't want to quit, but my husband's reaction was what troubled me the most. We had just gotten things on track with our marriage and now this comes up!

I called my job soon after and told them I wasn't coming back. I thanked them for everything they had done for me, but I still wasn't sure about my business. I knew without a shadow of a doubt that I was not making a mistake by quitting. Funny, that was the only clear thing on my mind. I was tired of trying to knock down a door that wouldn't budge.

The clock has started for me to figure out what I was going to do with my life…Yes, I had gotten several raises since I started, but never a promotion. I was ready and I believe I earned it. One of the ladies I had trained when she started with us, was getting promoted and I remember thinking this is my shot!

I looked at what these people had and what I did. I remember thinking what is more important, degrees, experience, history, tenure, what? Yes, I have the experience, history with the company, tenure, I was loyal, but no I didn't have a degree in business management.

I always wanted a degree in this subject, someday I pray to obtain it even now. I remember the day she announced her leave unofficially through office buzz. I kept putting my name in the air to her to express my interest. My husband always told me, "you gotta put yourself out there."

So I did, if there was something that needed to be done, training, helping someone, suggesting ideas, I did it all. What I didn't know I was quick to research to help be a part of a solution. I wanted this badly.

Chapter Seven

I remember the interview even now for this position. I walked into the building and I sat in my chair after I checked in with the receptionist. I wasn't incredibly confident as I didn't have all the education required. One thing I knew for sure, I was committed to doing whatever it took to get and keep this job. I know when I put my mind to something, there is not a resource I wouldn't read at the library to master my craft.

As I sat there, and to be honest, I started to bob my knee up and down slightly before I caught my nerves. Once I did, it was like my name was called and I was asked to come back. The person that invited me in was very well dressed. They had a sensible office, no windows or anything so I was a bit more nervous feeling like I was under a spotlight.

Before my nerves could overtake me, the interviewer says, "Hi Mrs. Devotis, how are you doing today? Did you find us alright?"

"Yes, thank you I did. I haven't been to this side of the building too often. Really not since I was hired almost 17 years ago. Thanks for having me," I replied.

"Well, it is our pleasure. We are always looking for good people, and hiring from within is our first priority. Also, looking over your resume and application, I would have wanted to call you in anyhow to see if there was some synergy. So tell me about yourself?"

"Well, I am a hard worker. I believe I work with excellence. I think what I do should be an example of who I am. I am solution-driven and focused on solving problems. I enjoy helping people and working with people."

I continued, "I have worked in customer service in several different capacities over the years. I am a team player, and there isn't much about this job I don't know. I make it my business to know as much as possible. So, I think I would make a good fit as the Customer Service manager."

"Okay, great. I see you worked for the postal service before coming to work with us?"

"Yes. I did. I enjoyed the work. I had a great reputation, and I have recommendations. I tend to keep long friendships, and I believe I have done a great job with being resourceful and bringing all my skills together here in this position."

The interviewer says, "That is true. I see you have many awards for outstanding service in your department. I also noticed you don't even have one reprimand on file."

"No, I have a supportive family. My husband supports my career goals and believes in me. I have reliable transportation, I show up on time, and I work hard. I think those three things are my best qualities. If I had to say my not so great quality, I am not the best on a computer at the start. I do believe I am a quick study, however, so the learning curve wouldn't be too much for me."

"Okay, there is training provided in this position. But I do want you to know, this position is salary and may include long days, or working weekends. You may also be required to travel for business functions and meetings. Would that be something you are still interested in?"

"Yes, I looked at the job description, and working a little bit more, traveling, is not a bad thing for me. I would like to think it a blessing in disguise."

"Okay, well, it was a pleasure to meet you Mrs. Devotis. I will be in touch with the next steps soon if you are selected. Is this still the best number to reach you on your resume and application?"

"Yes, it is," I replied as I got up from my chair. "Thanks so much for the interview and your time."

"As you go out do you mind telling the receptionist to hold the next few applicants for 10 or 15 minutes?"

"No, I don't mind at all. Have a wonderful day," I said as I disappeared from the room. I kept smiling the entire interview and I couldn't help it. I was happy in the hallway because I did my best! I am sure God will do it for me if it were meant, and I prayed it was.

As I got to the receptionist's desk to give the message, she replied, "Stay behind a sec will ya?"

"Of course," I said, unsure of what will happen next. Maybe I left something in the room? The receptionist then turns to the remaining applicants and announces, "I am grateful that you all have made it here today. We have your information here on file, but at this time, we have no more available positions. Should this change, we will reach back out to you, and best of luck with your search."

The last 3 applicants arose from their seats, some with sunken faces, others shaking their heads. The receptionist asks me, "Are you in a hurry? You got a few more minutes?"

"No, I am not in a hurry?"

"Okay great, follow me please." She walked me back to the back and I passed the office I interviewed in. I was walked to a much larger office with a window. Man the sun couldn't have been more perfect shining through the window. I then saw my interviewer again, my manager (Customer Service Manager), and then I was introduced to the director. He extended his hand and I accepted with a handshake.

My interviewer looked at me and said, "I had to bring Mrs. Devotis Lee down as she has been with the team for some time. She is an asset to our company and always going above and beyond."

I was happy, surprised, and shocked. I kept smiling at the director as he greeted me again and thanked me for my hard work. Wow, God did it!

As I got in my car to drive home I was still rehearsing the interview in my head. I knew the answers, I was prepared. I looked and felt great. Going home, I listened to some of my favorite gospel songs because I was truly happy. I had to share the news with my husband.

I knew my husband would be excited too for me. He knew how much I wanted this and he has always been a solid partner financially and otherwise in our family. I wanted to go vacationing and spend more time with him. More money from this promotion would help do that.

About a week later we were all gathered in the main room for a big announcement. I was surprised this day had come and I felt really good about the announcement. I was growing with anticipation these few days. My palms were sweating, and the room seemed to get small, yet I felt very alive as I awaited the news. I was ready and many of my coworkers were looking at me too because they knew how much I wanted this promotion.

As the Director came in and gave the introduction, thanking us for our commitment and service in this department. I clapped and could feel my energy mounting as he called up our Manager whom we knew was leaving.

"As you all know one of our jewels is leaving us to accept a position at another location. We are happy for her and we wish her the best of luck although we will miss her. With that being said, we have interviewed many of you in this office because we believe in promoting from within, and I want to tell you all thank you again for applying. Give yourself a round of applause."

The room entertained a clap and the silence quickly returned. His voice said, "Now after much review and consideration we would like to introduce to you, your next manager," I started to move to the edge of my seat.

"I want to welcome a newcomer to this location and to–" Instantly my mind cut off to whatever was coming next. Did he really just say a newcomer not only to our department but all together? What happened to hiring within? Did everything I do so far not even matter and was it considered?

As I saw another young person walk in front of me and stand next to our managers. I could feel my pressure mounting. I could hear my inner voice getting louder. The questions raising within me, the hurt, pain, and the shame didn't kick in until I realize the entire room was looking at me.

I was asked a question I missed, and my boss repeated himself, "Devotis we would love for you to show her the ropes, help her get caught up to speed. We know you are a valuable trainer in this department and if anyone can do this, it is you."

That was it, I am not sure I heard anything else after that. I don't remember seeing anyone else, feeling anything else…I blanked out right there at the office.

I was rushed to the hospital, the worst had happened not only in my mind but in my heart. I was heartbroken and a heart attack came with it. I never felt so embarrassed, so belittled, used. I was dying inside…

Chapter Eight

The first thing I learned before starting my business was everything I hated about where I was and what I wanted to change. It is scary when the head honcho doesn't like you anymore. It's like they hold the scissors and can cut your strings at any time watching you fall from the top to the bottom. The scary part, there is nothing you can do about it. I wanted off that string and I didn't want to feel I was selling my soul to merely survive.

I knew I wanted to ask for help and shine when I can. I wanted everyone to look and feel good about the business I started. I wasn't in the clique where I work but I wanted to establish a family within my business. I vowed to honor hard work and not put glass ceilings over people. I would believe in the importance of their dreams same as mine!

No matter who you are or where you come from, you can succeed because you are willing to work hard and laugh at your struggles. Winning is also being able to thank people and accept the next challenge. I was ready for my next challenge because of what I had already survived. I wanted to love what I do again.

On to the next challenge, I had to ask myself what do I love? At my previous job I didn't necessarily love what I did although I loved people. My newfound goal was to work with people and connect my passion for people with some kind of service. So what can I do that would involve customer service?

I think I thought about this for a few more weeks before I really knew what to do. I remember thinking about my mom and how she worked, cooked, cleaned, and always knew what to do to make us feel at home. Something my mom taught me to do that I used all the time that I didn't see as a business before. This simple thing, I did every night for my children and husband, on this day clicked in my head to become my business!

I've always loved to cook. Growing up it was a staple in our house for us all to learn to cook, because like making dresses, cooking at home was cheaper than going to restaurants or buying a dress off the rack. All of us had to learn to cook because my mother also saw it as a means of surviving. She knew if we wanted a family, and children, we must know how to cook. So she made us help her with dinner and breakfast all the time.

I've decided what I wanted to do, now I just have to find a way to tell my husband. I remember one night, he was going through the bills and asking me for an update on what I wanted to do next. I told him, "I want to go open my own restaurant!"

"What, a restaurant? You don't think we should think this threw a bit more? We are close to retirement and now you want to throw away the money on food? You do know this is the riskiest business any person can start?"

"Have a little faith. This will work."

"Dee, this is not a small deal. You need a building, staff, menus, furniture, and insurance. Those are all expenses. How can you think right now is the time for this? I think you are starting to lose it. Is this a midlife crisis?"

"No, it is none of those things. I just think we are young enough to take a risk. I always wanted to go into business, and now I can."

"But you have no experience! You cook at home, but you don't know anything about a commercial kitchen. Yes, you worked a job for years, but this is a whole new deal. This goes beyond customer service. You said you didn't want to work, but you are going to work double, triple scale probably with a restaurant."

"I think I have a plan. I will go and train with a chef to get my foundation. I think once I take a position, I am sure the rest will fill in over time."

"So you are going to go get a job now or start a business?"

"I will go get a job to start my business."

"So I can't talk you out of this?"

"I love you and this isn't something that is going away. I really want to do this and could use your support."

"Babe, I will always be here for you but I would be doing us a disservice if I didn't let you know that I am concerned. We have been working for a long time and I was expecting us to do a few more years together then we can travel. Starting this is like having a baby. We would be locked down to this business."

He continues to say, "I am not trying to rain on your parade Devotis, but what about us? I thought we were going to finally be able to party a bit, travel, and take it easy for a change. We've worked our entire lives, our children are gone. At this stage of our lives, we are supposed to finally be selfish."

"I know this isn't easy, but I really need this. Our versions of retirement may be a bit different right now, but they will align."

"I can't say I agree with your timing but if this is what you want to do, I will support you…"

This conversation was one of the most difficult things our marriage could bear at the time. This business was the topic of many debates moving forward. But I could not shake my passion. This passion perhaps led me blindly at times, but I don't regret the choice to start my business.

My husband has always loved me and he tried his best to support me. I knew he would give me the shirt off his back, and often he was the only one standing with me when everything did not go to plan. On this venture, it was a hard lesson to learn that some of our choices, and our choice to chase our dream, may mean some of that journey we walk alone.

My plan was shaky and yes I can understand my husband wanting to keep his name off documents, plans, and the business itself because we had to be safe. He wanted to give us a way out if we needed it. It would be hard for us to make it, if we both had bad credit or stumbled. Of course, he was also scared for me and scared of the potential I could fail. But this wasn't really about him, it was about me and accomplishing something I determined and set out to do.

Pulling out my 401k to start the business sounded scary to me too, but how else was I going to go after it? I had to now find a space, staff, and finalize a menu–I had to understand what owning a business would look like. Sure my uncle ran his own real estate business, but cooking and having a restaurant is a lot different than sitting in an office.

I felt out of my league but I knew the only thing I could do was pray. Pray that God leads me to the right people at the right time. I believe when God opens doors no one can close them. I loved my city of Atlanta and I knew what kind of food I wanted to make. I wasn't the person that knew a whole lot about location scouting, so I just prayed my way through it.

I remember riding around downtown and passing my old stomping ground. The area and part of town I grew up in. It was near Ralph David Abernathy. The street name has history and the area too. I remember passing on Ralph and seeing a shopping strip. I always liked seeing new businesses pop up and this area was good for change over every few years.

I saw an empty space and I almost hit my breaks in the middle of the street! I couldn't believe it. I parked in the side parking lot and walked up to the space with the sign. I saw that it was actually two empty spaces instead of one. But could this be in my budget, I remember thinking.

I wrote the number down, but I couldn't call it. Every time I looked at it, I got nervous. The Lord tells us not to be anxious about anything but to pray. So I prayed when I first saw the building. I didn't want to tell my husband my thoughts just yet because I knew the thought of having two spaces instead of one, would send him into overdrive.

Stress can cause strokes at our age, so we need to keep stress to a minimum. So I prayed and kept my desire between me and God. I drove by the space a few times and it was when I saw someone else walking out of the space, I knew I had to do something. So I picked up the phone and made a call.

Chapter Nine

I remember being so nervous, yet the person on the other end of the phone was cool as a cucumber. They didn't seem annoyed by my fumbling a bit through my introduction and questions. I am not sure why I got so nervous when I come to think about it. The worst that could happen was I get a no, and the best a yes, but the truth I wasn't sure which was good or bad at the time.

I asked how much it would cost to rent the space and how soon I could take a look inside. I was told others were also looking at the space so if I was interested I needed to come soon. The lady did mention that the next-door unit was available in case I was interested to rent both.

Arriving in that same parking lot and this

time thinking it possible to get keys was exciting. I said my prayer before I went to the door to meet the person showing me the place. The agent was very kind and he seemed like he knew a lot about the area. We did a bit of small talk before we went inside.

Going inside was not giving me butterflies. The space felt dark, cramp, and just didn't give me the happy vibe I wanted to feel. It was missing something. Although walking to the back I could see where the kitchen could go and how the front could work, but my vision was bigger. Have you ever dreamed of something big and it was hard for you to downsize?

So I asked to see next door also. I couldn't see this space before because it was paper up blocking the windows. As soon as I went inside I instantly felt it was right. The space was an open wide space. I could fit plenty of tables, host events, and really engage with the community on this side.

I shared my thoughts with the agent and he agreed the space would work best connected. Of course, he should say that as well because that meant he got a two-for-one deal. "The one side alone is a bit cramp for a restaurant, but the two together could work very well." Now it was time to talk numbers, honestly, I wish I had my husband or someone more experienced with me because I didn't know how to negotiate.

I wasn't really sure about what to ask, except, "Can I make changes to open the wall up?"

"Yes, you can easily connect these two spaces. You could even expose this brick since you keep saying how much you like it. It is behind all the walls in this building."

"Really?" I replied with enthusiasm. The agent kept talking and mentioning people they could recommend to help me build it out. He also didn't shy away from other potential persons that had spoken about leasing one or both sides. I didn't want to lose the space or risk having only one side. The two units together, fit my vision exactly.

My determination, or perhaps my blind passion, had me commit right then and there to both sides at the asking price. I know, I should have done my homework, but at the moment it just felt like the right thing to do. The only thing to do now was to pull the money from my 401k. Telling my husband I was getting a restaurant was a difficult conversation, but this may have him lose it!

I pulled the money from my 401k. Honestly, I pulled it all out because I also needed money for my renovations, staff, menus and so more stuff I was sure. I really wasn't sure what I would need but I knew it all cost money.

After obtaining the building, I did think some of the hard work was behind me. The renovations I had in mind were approved, and I wasn't picking up a hammer so I thought the renovation would simply go as scheduled. I was new to a lease and new to construction. One thing I underestimated was the age of the building.

Have you ever jumped in feet first only to take a deeper and closer look later? When walls started to get busted up I was excited at first. I saw the open concept, I can envision the paint changing, I loved the exposed brick; but I didn't realize items like replumbing, rewiring, and replacing structural things would creep into my design budget. It is one thing when you set a budget for what you want to spend and stick to it.

I remember when I told my husband the budget, talk about sticker shock! We both hadn't seen as much money as I spent at one time ever up until that point. I remember my husband going through the space, seeing the work, and shaking his head. He told me, "You are doing too much for a building you don't own. We are risking too much on a business where your clients may not have the money to afford your prices."

My husband used to ask, "Do you think people could afford to pay your prices Devotis? I mean we have to be sure you are not shortchanging yourself. Some people pretend like they will help you, but when you open they ain't there. I don't want to see you hurt."

I always felt he was wrong about the black dollar and I always believed my food could appeal to more than just black people anyhow. Soul food gets a bad wrap around the world for being unhealthy, undesirable, or fattening. I worked hard on my menu to combine health, taste, imagination, and soul.

This is a part of our history I often thought that shouldn't be thrown away. Why do we have to throw away our history to pick up someone else's cuisine to be successful? I enjoy food from all over the world, and I see how many cultures have embraced soul food in their own way too. I wanted to take my experiences and do the same thing but from my point of view.

I knew I was asking my husband for a lot, but I never had to ask him to love or be committed to me. The first few months of construction were tiresome. Our plan to be opened was pushed back because of additional repairs I had to make. It seemed like every few steps forward was at least one backward.

Within the first few weeks of construction, I quickly realized how fast money was flowing, and not so much in my direction. I needed to get a job first to learn and secondly to earn some extra cash while the renovations were underway. I was not a professionally trained cook but I always knew my way around the kitchen. I planned to start my menu with my home classics, but I was not at all familiar with running the business side.

I applied to several restaurants and I landed an $11 an hour job as a cook. I was grateful for that job. I never thought I would get so much enjoyment from going to work. The hours were long and the work tiresome. I never complained because I saw this as my college training. It is a beautiful thing when you can get paid to learn.

The only drawback to getting paid to learn is when you forget the goal at hand. I was on the job for about a month, and my store was set to open in a month. I knew if I wanted to be successful I would have to be present and direct my team. I never planned on being at the job full time.

Imagine my shock when I was offered a $60k a year position with the restaurant about two weeks before my planned exit and intended notice being given. It was hard for me to tell my husband how I was going to turn it down. He was happy about the offer, but that wasn't my plan. With the setbacks, we were having and issues in our marriage, this job would have looked like an answer to prayer.

Only it wasn't an answer to prayer, I saw it as a roadblock to living my dream. Have you ever felt so stressed, heavy with a decision you literally paced the floor as you prayed? I did that before telling my husband I gave my two weeks and turned down the job. He was flabbergasted! I always wanted to use that word and on that day, it fit perfectly to describe his reaction.

Our marriage was surely tested at this moment and I encourage everyone to prepare their family for the challenges that starting a new business brings. The first few months were brutal because making money wasn't on the radar. I had to do construction, work on menus, find staff, and pay associated bills. I loved the idea of working for myself, but getting paid last was a challenge. I still hadn't made a penny yet, and that was the case for several more months after!

You have heard people say, "pay yourself first." This was surely not meant in the context of opening a new business. Perhaps more so of what you do when you get paid; but what if that is skipped for several months? It has happened to me. So what did I do to get through?

Chapter Ten

I leaned on family, my husband for sure, and professionals. I am quick to admit I don't know everything, and at times even what I thought I knew changed. I realized although it was my dream, my ability to accomplish it required input from other people. Never believe that your dream is only limited to making you happy. The best dreams always include other people.

So I started my hiring process beginning first by looking at talented individuals I knew first. I believe in building family or generational wealth. I also believe that hiring family can ruin a great thing if they abuse that relationship. Striking a balance of respect is crucial. I was able to start by hiring my children. It is amazing how the young babies we raise can grow up and teach us so much as parents isn't it?

I didn't know as much as them when it came to computers or social media. These two fairly new concepts were intimidating for me in the beginning. I struggled with releasing some control because I worried, 'would this change my dream?' Sometimes we can hold on too tight to our dream that we don't allow it to grow. Let your vision grow by trusting the talent you have selected.

I knew that none of my family or personnel I hired wanted to hurt me, but that didn't mean it wouldn't happen. I had to be open to strong criticism in the beginning, even still now. Being open to ideas has helped me make necessary changes to launch and expand my business. Those ideas that I thought at the beginning were very different from what I envisioned, some proved to work out very well. Like social media.

I appreciate how my family invested their skills, time, and abilities in my dream. They gave me the confidence I needed to speak to new customers and also hire staff I didn't know already. I remember hiring my first non-family member employees. It was a pair of twins.

The twins were both challenged, in that they suffered from legitimate handicaps. Yet this beautiful girl and boy twin pair wanted a chance to do what other kids did, work! I admire hard work and

I love it when people don't make excuses for why they can't do something. These twins were in high school when they started and they stayed with me up until they graduated.

It was a blessing to them and their family for them to have their jobs. I realized, that being an employer you can make a real difference in people's lives. You can help them take care of their children. Support their parents, and even help with pocket change so they could do and buy things they wanted. I was so impressed by them, that I found myself doing for them things they never asked. I can admit, it is a challenge for me to cut off given at times, but I never regretted a single thing I did for them.

When you have employees, as the owner, you are invested in them. You have to make sure you make money or have it, so you can pay them. If your business fails, you fail, but also they fail and whoever is attached to them. I started to realize the responsibility I had by employing the twins. I also saw it with my children, because my grandchildren needed me to win.

I was more afraid of letting people down that needed me and desired to help me than going out of business. I always had a servant's heart and a desire to see people achieve. Growing up, I was very busy in the civic space and that gave rise to me wanting to go into business. Yes, I had my challenges with corporate America and I wanted to change that narrative.

I wanted to know what it was like to be the lender and not always the borrower. To be the owner and not always the employee. When I got the chance I took it and never looked back. Sure I wished I would have been a bit wiser on things, but I am now. We learn from our mistakes and our experiences. My experiences prepared me to get here, and also encouraged me to keep going.

Don't allow your prediction of what will go right or wrong to stop you from trying. It is in the process of going through that we come out with the golden nuggets for success. Sometimes to learn to win, we first have to understand what failed. Patience is needed when starting something new, because there is always a learning curve, no matter what you do. Try to consider the cost as much as possible and be realistic about that cost so you can fund your growth and learning curve as much as possible.

Residing in what is known today as "Hot Lanta," comes with its perks if you are an up-and-coming minority business owner. It is no secret how much black wealth has been amassed in this city. They call it chocolate city too, but it hasn't always been a utopia for melanated people.

I remember growing up in this southern state of Georgia and witnessing many differences between myself and others. I had friends of all social levels within the all-black schools I attended. Some were from families with professionals as parents and others did not. What I noticed, we all went through the color test when applying for jobs.

I consider myself always a very smart person that is also pleasant, friendly, and I had the skills to secure a great job. Out of school, I didn't have the grades I needed to be as impressive. I did not go straight to college after finishing, so I knew I was a risk for certain positions.

A good friend of mine from school, who was darker than I, but who had more education and better grades applied for the same job as me. We were both going for a receptionist position at a local business. We would be the first face customers would see. She told me before we heard back from applying that I had a better chance of getting hired than she did.

Your look and appearance were part of the process. Before they saw your skills, the employer saw your face, skin tone, and attire. You were a package deal and some companies struggled with these natural attributes that I wanted to believe weren't the case. I desired to see a flaw in her reasoning, but I am not sure that she has been proven incorrect.

Unlike today where your image can be

delayed from being revealed, back in the day it was unavoidable. All around, on paper, and purely on skill, grades, and experience my friend outpaced me. I didn't believe her when she said that to me. I looked at the hard facts because I am a realist. I had no professional training. I needed some help with understanding and using computers. As you may have picked up, I was never really tech-savvy even when I was younger. I also wear glasses and she didn't–but maybe that made me look smart?

After we both were seen, I was offered the job. My friend was not offered that job but one that paid less at the same company. She sat at a desk toward the back of the department and I felt so bad because I feared for her future. If this is happening now, what could she–will she go through over a lifetime I remember thinking.

It is no secret that color played a role in how some people, even in black communities, defined beauty. Some people had the talk, the conversation where you couldn't bring anyone home that was the shade of an iron skillet or darker than a cup of cappuccino. Others were told slogans to appreciate certain men, like "the blacker the berry, the sweeter the juice."

Or nicknames like redbone, red, or chocolate could be thought of as terms of endearment–but not for everyone. These terms made us see our shade the more vividly and some cared to be lighter or darker. There are stereotypes in our community about people with darker skin. Some feel like the darker you are the angrier you could get or the likelihood you would be mean. Blackness is associated with aggression. For a spell, many darker skin women hated their complexion because they felt lighter women were more favored.

Similar thoughts were believed about hair texture, and how good hair is defined. These ideas and social norms that crept into our society by way of images or standards that were set to define beauty based on the most influential society's viewpoint have caused damage to those who don't fit the viewpoint. Many who were outside of the standards would feel isolation, shame, or not feel desired.

If you don't feel desired romantically, you are marginalized at work, and it can make you critical of yourself internally. This perception of oneself is a recipe for destruction. Many men and especially women, I can speak more to this being one myself, go through self-doubt and insecurities. We are constantly comparing ourselves to each other and not always for the best reasons.

Insecurities are formed when a person hears someone else say something about them. Insecurities would never materialized if a person didn't value the opinions of the wrong person at one time. Our desire to please, be accepted, or included will have some push their limits.

Sometimes people think being overly aggressive in what they can control, will help them feel better about what they can't. If you can't protect your family outside, you may abuse your power inside the house to prevent danger outside. With the recent uptick in interest among people around the world for how black people live in America, it has shed a light on injustices long past. Likewise, it highlights how some things haven't changed or need to change a whole lot more!

Chapter Eleven

Women have fought for rights for a very long time. We have led several movements for voters' rights, equal pay, and as of late representation within political offices or high-level corporate positions. In the Biden administration this is the first time in history a woman–and yes even a woman of cultural descent, has held such a high position in this country. Never did many think they would see a day when a woman would run for president and let alone a black woman would have a chance at being vice president of the United States of America.

We have come a long way from when a woman's job was predominately domestic. When my mother was young she didn't teach me ambitions to excel corporately, she taught me how to keep a household, work with my hands, and take care of my children. She did a great job and I was grateful, but I wanted to be an FBI agent when I was a child. I had nobody to help me achieve that, especially being a woman because my grandmother was a maid and my mom worked in a hospital. Their career fields were very different from mine.

I would never say I am ashamed of my grandmother, what she did for a living being a maid, or that I wanted a different upbringing. I just wished there were more outlets for me to become comfortable walking in the role I am in today. I wished there were avenues to help women or girls achieve something that is outside the ordinary.

I feel like the old saying that women don't know much about mechanics and cars is still a widely accepted idea. Women are still underrepresented in engineering, the medical field, science, politics, and senior-level management positions. Women still have a nationwide view of being the weaker vessel, as described in the Bible also, but women are strong in areas too!

With the right support, help, and training, we can stand tall in positions we were once not welcomed to the table before. When I started this business I do feel I was taken advantage of. I was not as savvy in business which also didn't make it easier. I found myself feeling like I had to be nice to be liked or respected.

When I felt cheated I didn't want to come off as an emotional woman. Passion or excitement can be misunderstood for women in business. Likewise, there are stereotypes about the angry black female. If anyone knows a thing about stereotypes, most good people like to prove them wrong. In trying to prove them wrong, it can backfire to the point where we are so busy proving something to someone else, we leave ourselves exposed.

I did not cover myself and my investment like I should have. I came into business with a mothering spirit. I wanted to take care of people, be a family, and do what mothers do. What I realized, sometimes we can have disobedient or ungrateful children. These children are difficult because you have to love them at a distance.

I think one of the hardest things for me to learn in business, was to love people at a distance. To separate them as people and see them as employees also. When you work with someone every day and learn about their family, you may be tempted to take on their burdens. Building bonds can be a hazard if the bond stops you from doing your job or looking out for your company's best interest.

You may not fire someone because you understand how that may impact their children. But what about you? Your business? Many would say, oh you will be okay. But many new startups close within their first two years. I know all these owners weren't just bad managers, poor handlers of money, or mean people.

Some of these people struggled with trying to have people like or love them in hopes they would be loyal and work for them. One of the things I learned in business that applies to many other things is "always look for a win, win." We can't hold anyone in place or make them stay with us forever. We have to allow them to grow and even move on.

I hired employees that worked for me faithfully when in high school, but after, they had to transition and I lost a great team member. I was of course happy for them, but I also realized, I had to plan my business with change in mind. If I ran my business like a family some things I would inherently never prepare for. Does a child ever think their mother or father would abandon them? Do parents really think about how when their child grows up they will move out and get their own family?

Do we really comprehend how our relationships change as they grow? As business owners, we have to anticipate those changes for our business. I had to learn, the same way as we do with parenting, that people will grow up, elevate, and desire more or different things. With these changes, my business has to survive and be able to move on also. I in fact want to do more things than run my business. I want to travel and finally spend more time with my husband.

I also enjoy public speaking and would like to connect my two passions: speaking and traveling. When I started this journey I wasn't sure where I was going. I don't regret my choices, but I wish I did a few things differently. I was happy that I took some time off during the Obama election to volunteer.

As many have heard, voting numbers went through the roof in his second election. I wanted to be a part of history, and do my civic duty of helping my fellow man. I went to the southern region of Georgia/Florida to help black voters who were being disenfranchised. I had always been an advocate for representation. Within my store, I have hung many pictures that document my participation.

I have catered mayoral race campaign dinners, donated time to people's campaigns, opened my restaurant up for community meetings, and even allowed pop-up boutiques to take over for a day or week at a time. I believe in supporting people that are trying to change the narrative for our communities. This is something I must make time for or I will miss this chance in life.

Going further south and seeing the glaring difference in poll locations lit a fire in me. The voter suppression of some locals not allowing people to sign up or use their ideas, just really finding any small fault to turn them away was eye-opening. I remember back in the '60s when it was extremely difficult to express your desire to vote. Now people appear to be intimidated or feel the system doesn't work, so they don't show up.

It is sad for me to see so many who just wouldn't come down because they had a bad experience in the past. They permitted that experience to rob them of their involvement in obtaining representation. I believe change comes by getting involved. Yes, it doesn't all rest on politicians and the government, but some of it does. All people should be able to use their rights in this country regardless of their skin color to obtain fair and necessary justice.

Sweeping things under the rug will leave a very big pile that must be addressed. To think of the numbers booming the way they did and to know that so many didn't even show up to the poles is astounding. I would like to speak more on this topic of community involvement, and how it is our duty to vote. Our children need our votes and many of our ancestors died to get them for us. If we don't vote for no other reason, I think these two reasons are more than enough.

I also have to admit that politics and representation have helped women at large. When I thought of starting my business even a handful of years ago, the resources were not as many as they are today. There are several large corporations offering specialty management training to women-owned businesses. Consulting scholarships are now also being handed out to these businesses.

I am glad to be born in a time such as this because the sky is really the limit. If you can dream of something and are willing to work for it, you can achieve it. I am a living witness, you don't even need to know everything. You can make mistakes and still win, but if you don't have to make the same errors to learn, don't!

If I had to do things over again, I would not have put so much of my money into my business. I used my entire 401k to repair a building that I don't own. Although at the time my husband said it, I didn't want to believe he was right. I wished I would have heard the good things I needed in his caution and not only have chosen to hear his doubt.

Sometimes people can be saying the right things to us, we just don't want to accept it. In this case, he was right. I shouldn't have gone broke like I did. In the first few years, I didn't take vacations either. I worked every day and it felt like all day. My marriage went from rocky to a stoney place. I really didn't have more time for my family but less. It would have been more ideal to be on the same page as my husband and have more expertise so everything wasn't on me at the start.

I know many people run away from coaches, consultants, and expertise. We think oh, I don't need their help. They just want my money. I can tell you, if I would have spent a few thousand dollars on a good coach, I could have saved tens of thousands of dollars. I would have known some factors about the building. I would have moved slower because I would have talked my ideas over with someone.

I really went into this alone from a business standpoint, and that was a mistake. I didn't think about getting a loan or using credit to start my business. Like many of you, I felt I wouldn't qualify. I later found, that if I would have worked on my credit, I could have gotten funded and used credit to launch. I didn't understand finances. Really, I am still not so savvy.

I had introductions to finance over my lifetime, but nothing prepared me to run a business–not even my internship! Every business is different and comes with its own challenges. My business was no different.

Chapter Twelve

I went to a lot of classes trying to educate myself, but remember I am a new business owner trying to build my entire team. What I picked up from my family, as a learned lesson, was how to save. When I worked for the packaging company, I saved 6 dollars a week every week. I was amazed at how committed I was to saving and I loved the return. I didn't think I could do it, but I did and I taught that to my children.

To have seen my 401k all those years later was breath taken. I had never seen so much money at one time before starting this business. It makes me wonder, how much more would I have saved if I knew this day would actually come? Money does better when you invest. I used to have stocks, not so much now, although I think I may pick it up again. I really appreciate that I bought savings bonds for my children and I instilled this lesson into them too.

My daughter is especially a pro when it comes to savings, coupons, and keeping her money longer. I wish I would have learned more about credit and leveraging money besides knowing only to use my own. Most people that are wealthy I am learning are investors, not simply savers. I would like to do more investing as I expand my financial profile.

I will also say this, being in my community, it is always rewarding when I get recognized for what I do. My goal is and will always be representation. I wanted to start this business to show myself and my community that a black woman can accomplish great things. I can run a business and do it well my way.

Yes, I am still learning, but I created a menu I am proud of. I have created a culture within my restaurant and catering business that I can stand by. This matters to me and I want to be sure I stay true to myself too! In being true, you will find you will achieve what you desire.

I wanted to build a name and shine a positive light on a minority-owned business. Since I have been in business these past 5 years, I have received many awards and acknowledgments. I received an honorary mention from the Red Cross.

I also received an acknowledgment and cash prize from DoorDash in 2020!

A blood supplier told me I would make history for bringing my old company to work with the Red Cross. I didn't know that one blood donation could save 6 lives! When I heard what one donation could do, and I knew that there were 300 plus people at every location, it only seemed right to get involved. We helped the Red Cross understand the importance of establishing a partnership with these corporate entities. They told me I would be mentioned in their history because of my contribution to how they received donations.

Some of our greatest rewards aren't money but being recognized for what we do or simply being appreciated. DoorDash also saw the quality of my food and desired to highlight my business. It was an honor that in all of Atlanta, a shop off Ralph David Abernathy made it onto their radar. Business has jumped since the feature and I am so grateful. We are even working on expanding the open space into a bar area.

I also wanted something like a neighborhood hangout. I used to watch a show when I was younger that established this vibe and I wanted the same neighborly feeling here. I always wanted to create that same energy and comfort in my business. Where everyone knows your name because you're family. Although I am grateful for everything happening now in my life, this success didn't happen overnight; it has been a process.

There have been good and bad things that have happened and both led to great results. My team for one had to be patient through the not-so-good times, so great can manifest. I would say that one of my finest accomplishments was not just what I did with my business, but how I helped to support other companies. I was happy to help launch a black-owned delivering company by being one of their newest and first clients!

For everyone that has worked for me, helped me build, and those helping to keep it together, thank you! No business runs without a great team. Never underestimate your team! They truly are the foundation and your greatest support.

Of course, without customers, why would you go into business? I think having a passion to serve or solve a problem has to be the cornerstone of any good business. If you are thinking of starting a business, think of a problem and then solve it. In short, be a problem solver! I saw that there were very few cafes that sold healthy soul food alternatives. I wanted to prove that soul food isn't bad food or junk food only.

I also saw a need to have other ethnic foods represented in a community so vast. Atlanta is a melting pot like any great city. I saw every kind of cuisine with dozens if not 100s of options, but only a handful in my space.

It's also okay not to know what you want to do and allow yourself time to figure it out. Getting a coach or bouncing ideas around is a good idea too! I benefited greatly from the Small Business Association. I had meetings often and today I have a coach also. Don't be afraid to ask for help. It doesn't make you less professional but all the wiser. Nobody builds a city on their lonesome. Dream big! Then make preparations to win. You can do this just like I have.

Oh, and for those who think it is too late, it is not! Age is not a factor when you dream. I started this business a few years before retirement age. I wasn't taking care of myself before and honestly, I got worse when I started my business. I did miss quality time with my husband, but God has a way of bringing things into perspective.

I realized, we only live once. If you have a bucket list, go for it! If there are things you want to do, do them! I was able to travel to China, Hawaii, Canada, Jamaica, South America, Panama Canal, and many other places. I am glad I did because I had a major surgery in 2020 that would alter my travel plans.

My surgery involved removing my spleen and crazy enough, some countries won't let you visit without it. Smile. Good thing, some of the countries on this list that I wanted to visit, I had already been! I took many months off in 2020 to enjoy some things I was missing all these years. One of the things we all can take for granted is the people that stand by our side–thick or thin.

I really have to say a special thanks to my husband, children, siblings, and their children (my grandchildren). They really have supported me in everything I have ever done and I only pray they feel the same about me. I would love to share the goodness of family and God with the world. I do believe we all have something inside of us that the world can benefit from.

I would of course like to tell God first thank you! Thank you for allowing me to help people that are like me, wanting to start something new. I love to encourage and lift people up because I know what it takes to stay focused and motivated. I want people to learn from me and overcome their challenges like how I am learning also. If the challenges are age, race, gender, identity, or self-confidence, you can overcome them all.

About the Author

Devotis Lee, the owner of D Cafe in Atlanta Georgia, is a talented chef and established community advocate. Born October 11,1957 to Julius and Margaret Griffin in Atlanta, Georgia. Devotis has always known she was destined for greatness and wanted a family.

Mrs. Lee has three children, two step-children, a loving husband, and grandchildren that love her so much. In addition to running her restaurant and catering business, Devotis is excited about authoring books, traveling, and speaking about her life experiences to help others.

Soon, she plans to publish more books, volunteer in more civic duties including voting and political initiatives, and travel to speak to new business owners or people that need encouragement. Mrs. Lee has always had a passion to live life to the fullest and she believes age should not change that ambition.

She currently resides in the Atlanta Metro area with her husband.

YOU Have a STORY

Have you been inspired by an Author?

YOU have **A Story**! What's **YOURS**?

KLE Publishing specializes in helping people become authors. In as little as 90 days, we can help you develop your book and publish to 39,000 outlets!

We help **YOU** Structure, Edit, Format And can even write it for **YOU!**

Finance options available. No Credit Check or Minimum Score required to quaify.

770-240-0089 Ext 1